Cell Function and Specialization

Lori Johnson

Raintree

Chicago, Illinois

Customer Service 888-454-2279
Visit our website at www.heinemannraintree.com

Editorial: Megan Cotugno, Andrew Farrow, and Clare Lewis
Design: Philippa Jenkins
Illustrations: KJA-artists.com
Picture Research: Ruth Blair
Production: Alison Parsons
Originated by Modern Age
Printed and bound in China by Leo Paper Group

13 12 11
10 9 8 7 6 5 4 3 2

Library of Congress Cataloging-in-Publication Data
Johnson, Lori.
 Cell function and specialization / Lori Johnson.
   p. cm. -- (Sci-hi: life science)
 Includes bibliographical references and index.
 ISBN 978-1-4109-3238-9 (hc) -- ISBN 978-1-4109-3253-2 (pb) 1. Cells. I. Title.
 QH582.5.J6388 2008
 571.6--dc22
                    2008027373

Acknowledgments
The author and publishers are grateful to the following for permission to reproduce copyright material: © Corbis/Charles E. Rotkin p. **21**; © Corbis/Jim Zuckerman p. **8**; © Corbis/Lester V. Bergman p. **40**; © Corbis/MedicalRF.com p. **18**; © Corbis/Visuals Unlimited pp. **5, 16, 22**; © Corbis/Winston Luzier/Transtock pp. **iii** (Contents, bottom), **23**; © Getty Images/Stone p. **27**; © iStockphoto/Phil Morley background images and design features throughout; © naturepl.com/Eric Baccega p. **33**; © naturepl.com/Francois Savigny p. **4**; © naturepl.com/Kim Taylor p. **6**; © Photolibrary Group/Fancy p. **6**; © Photolibrary Group/Image100 p. **28**; © Photolibrary Group/Wiki Shots p. **31**; © Science Photo Library/Andrew Syred p. **41**; © Science Photo Library/Astrid & Hanns-Frieder Michler p. **25**; © Science Photo Library/CNRI p. **14** (bottom) © Science Photo Library/Dr. Kari Lounatmaa pp. **iii** (Contents, top), **7**; © Science Photo Library/Dr. Nigel Burton p. **9**; © Science Photo Library/Eye of Science pp. **20**; © Science Photo Library/John Durham p. **17**; © Science Photo Library/National Cancer Institute p. **37**; © Science Photo Library/Omikron p. **14** (top); © Science Photo Library/Pasieka p. **36**; © Science Photo Library/Steve Gschmeissner pp. **13, 19, 35**; © Science Photo Library/Zephyr p. **29**.

Cover photographs reproduced with permission of © Corbis/Lester V. Bergman **main**; © Science Photo Library/Andrew Syred **inset**.

The publishers would like to thank literacy consultants Nancy Harris, Patti Suerth, and Monica Szalaj, and content consultant Dr. Michelle Raabe for their assistance in the preparation of this book.

Some words are shown in bold, **like this**. These words are explained in the glossary. You will find important information and definitions underlined and in bold, **like this**.

Contents

What Is a Cell?   4

The Discovery of Cells   6

Inside a Cell   10

A Cell's Covering   16

Cell Movement   18

Types of Cells   20

Organisms   24

Cells and Energy   26

Respiration   28

Photosynthesis   30

Cell Growth and Division   32

Specialized Cells   36

Cell Function Review   42

Quiz   43

Glossary   44

Further Information   47

Index   48

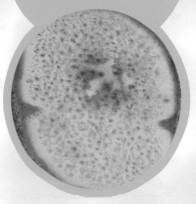

Bacteria like this were some of the first to be viewed under a microscope.

Learn more on page 7.

What function do cells have in keeping crops free of harmful insects?

Find out on page 23.

What Is a Cell?

What do a tiger, grass, and an oak tree have in common? They are all made up of **cells**. In fact, every living thing on Earth is made up of cells. <u>**A cell is a tiny unit that is the basic building block of life.**</u> Most cells are so small that they cannot be seen with the human eye.

The work of cells

Cells perform many jobs, such as building **proteins** and releasing **energy**. Plant and animal cells do similar jobs, although there are some differences in their structures. Cells come in different shapes and sizes depending on the job they do.

Like every living thing, both a tiger and a blade of grass are made of cells.

Cells are not just hidden inside a living thing like a candy inside a wrapper. Instead, cells are the material that actually makes up a living thing, just as a brick wall is made of bricks.

MANY TINY CELLS

The human body is made up of about 10 trillion cells. Side by side, 2,000 cells from the human body would cover about 2 centimeters squared (less than one square inch).

The Discovery of Cells

How do scientists know so much about **cells** if they are too small to see? The invention of the microscope made it possible for people to learn about very small objects, including cells. Before the microscope, people did not even know that cells existed.

This dog flea has been magnified 50-60 times under a light microscope.

The lenses of a light microscope are similar to the curved pieces of glass found in eyeglasses. The lenses magnify an object by bending the light that passes through them.

Early microscopes

The invention of the light microscope around 1590 allowed people to discover cells. The light microscope uses **lenses** to focus light and make a small object appear larger. Over the years, the light microscope has been improved so that it can magnify an object up to 1,500 times its normal size.

First observations of cells

Robert Hooke and Anton van Leeuwenhoek both used light microscopes to discover cells in the 1600s. In 1663 Robert Hooke noticed rectangular spaces in cork, which is from a special type of tree called the Cork Oak. Hooke called these spaces *cells*, which mean small rooms.

When Anton van Leeuwenhoek looked at lake water under a light microscope, he saw one-celled **organisms** that moved. Some of these organisms became known as **protozoa**.

Bacteria were some of the first cells to be viewed under a microscope. The bacteria shown here have been magnified 24,000 times!

How tiny is a microscopic object?

When you observe an object under a microscope, it's important to understand how tiny the size of the structures really is. The following table gives some conversions that might help you:

1 millimeter (mm) = 0.039 inch (in)

1 micrometer (μm) = 0.000039 inch (in)

1 nanometer (nm) = 0.000000039 inch (in)

Modern microscopes

Many structures within a cell are too small to be seen with a light microscope. The development of the **electron microscope** in the 1930s made it possible for scientists to see most of these structures. An electron microscope can enlarge images up to 500,000 times or more. This type of microscope uses a beam of **electrons** instead of light to make a magnified picture. Electrons are extremely small particles or pieces of matter.

With an electron microscope, you can see the small details on this flea leg!

Seeing with Sound

Sound waves can be used to see cells! An **acoustic microscope** uses sound waves instead of light or electrons to create a picture of a cell. With an acoustic microscope, doctors can examine cells for cancer without removing the cells from the person's body.

The cell theory

After the discoveries of Hooke and Leeuwenhoek, other researchers began using microscopes to learn about cells. In the 1800s, three German scientists added to people's understanding about cells. Their ideas became known as the **cell theory**. The cell theory states that:

• All living things are made of one or more cells.
• The cell is the smallest unit of life.
• All cells are produced from other cells.

This is an acoustic microscopic image of an onion cell. It was taken using sound waves, instead of light!

Inside a Cell

Cells are like tiny factories where **chemical reactions take place**. Put very simply, a chemical reaction is when matter changes its properties. These reactions happen in a gel-like substance inside a cell called **cytoplasm**. <u>**In most cells a structure called the nucleus controls all the activity in the cell.**</u> The following picture shows the inside of an animal cell.

Cytoplasm

The inside of a cell is filled with cytoplasm. Cytoplasm is a thick, gelatin-like fluid made of water and protein. Materials can move around the cell easily because the cytoplasm is constantly in motion.

Cytoskeleton

Cells do not have a skeleton of bones inside. Instead, cells contain a network of fibers in the cytoplasm called the cytoskeleton. The cytoskeleton is like a thick web that helps the cell keep its shape.

Nucleus

The control center of the cell is called the nucleus. The nucleus directs the cell's functions.

Golgi apparatus
(see page 15)

Ribosome
(see page 14)

Cell Membrane
(see page 16)

Mitochondria
(see page 14)

11

Why is the nucleus important?

The nucleus contains genetic material, the chemical instructions that tell the cell what to do. The **nucleus** is surrounded by a membrane that protects the genetic material inside.

DNA

The genetic material in the nucleus that contains instructions for cell function is called **DNA (deoxyribonucleic acid)**. The DNA also carries information about an organism's characteristics. This information is passed from parent to offspring.

Genes

DNA is made up of **genes**. Genes tell the cell what proteins to produce. **Proteins** help determine the size, shape, and color of an organism as well as other traits.

DNA IN EVIDENCE

Each person's DNA is unique and different from everyone else's DNA. People who investigate crimes use DNA found in saliva, blood, and skin cells to connect the criminal to the crime scene. The DNA information is used in court cases as strong evidence.

WOW!

The nucleus of the average human cell is extremely small, yet each one contains almost 1.8 meters (6 feet) of DNA. To avoid tangles, the DNA is wound around proteins like thread around a spool.

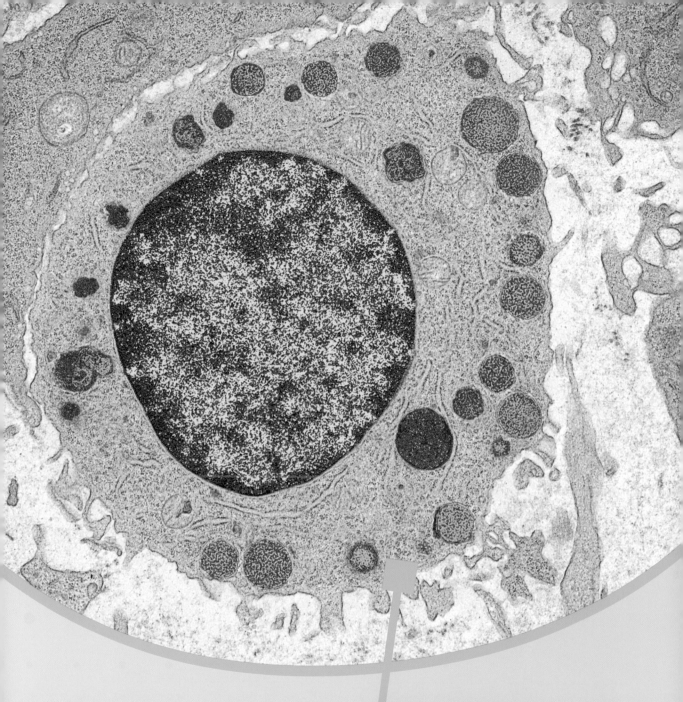

Above is an electron microscope image of a white blood cell. The large, bright orange spot is the cell's nucleus.

Organelles

Structures in charge of chemical reactions float in the cytoplasm of a cell. These structures are called **organelles**. Each organelle performs a specific function so that the cell can make proteins and other substances. They also help the cell use **energy** and store materials.

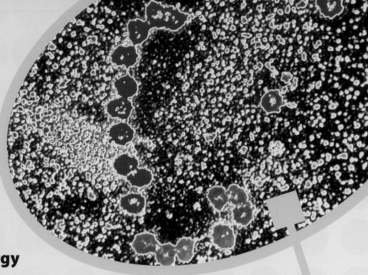

The round, red images (above) are ribosomes.

Building proteins

Cells make important **molecules** called proteins. Proteins are built inside small structures called **ribosomes**. Proteins are important for cell repair.

Using energy

The chemical reactions that change energy in food to energy the cell uses for power happen in the **mitochondria**. These rod-shaped structures are the power plants of the cell. Most plants can make their own food to use for energy. This happens in green organelles called **chloroplasts**.

The rod-shaped purple structures in this photo are mitochondria.

Moving and storing materials

The **Golgi apparatus** is also part of a cell. It processes materials for the cell. It receives and modifies (changes) products from the **rough endoplasmic reticulum (RER)** and the **smooth endoplasmic reticulum (SER)**.

The large sac floating in the cytoplasm of a plant cell is the **vacuole**. It stores food, water, and waste products. Some animal cells contain a vacuole. Others do not.

The following chart lists the parts of a cell, their functions, and in what type of cell they are found.

Cell structure	Function	Cell type
cytoskeleton	cell shape	all cells
nucleus	controls cell functions	all animal and plant cells
ribosome	produces protein	all cells
mitochondrion	releases energy	most cells except bacteria
chloroplast	makes food	most plant cells
Golgi apparatus	stores, changes, and transports molecules	most cells except bacteria
vacuole	stores water and plant substances	plant and some animal cells

A CELL'S COVERING

How do the parts of a **cell** stay together? <u>**All cells have a special outer covering that holds the cell together and keeps the cell safe.**</u> Although both plant and animal cells have this covering, plant cells have an extra structure on the outside called a **cell wall**.

Cell membrane

All cells have a **cell membrane**. The cell membrane is the thin, flexible covering that surrounds the cell. This membrane protects the inside of the cell from harmful materials. The membrane has openings that control what substances can get into and out of a cell.

Cell wall

Some cells, such as those in plants, have a stiff cell wall that surrounds the cell membrane. The cell wall is made mostly of **cellulose**, a material containing tough fibers. These fibers in the cell wall support the cell and give the cell its stiff shape.

You can see the cell membrane (dark pink) surrounding the animal cell in this photo.

A plant's cell walls surround the chloroplasts, which contain green chlorophyll.

CELL WALL PAPER

Students write on cellulose every day! The cellulose found in plant cell walls has been used to make paper for almost 2,000 years. Cellulose is separated from wood by grinding wood chips underwater. Then the cellulose is washed, bleached, and poured over a screen to drain. The web of fibers left behind becomes a sheet of paper after it is dried and pressed.

Cell Movement

Under a microscope, some **cells** appear to hop, twist, and swim. Just as animals use legs, wings, or fins to move, cells may have **appendages** to make movement possible. <u>An appendage is a structure, or part, attached to the outside of the cell. Not all cells have appendages or need to move.</u>

Flagellum

A **flagellum** is a long, tail-like appendage connected to the outside of single-celled organisms and sperm. This appendage moves a cell forward by lashing back and forth like a whip. The appendage can also move in a circular motion, like a boat propeller.

A sperm cell uses its flagellum to move toward a female egg.

Cilia

Cilia are short, hair-like appendages. Cilia usually occur in large numbers on a cell. The wave-like motion of cilia can move the cell around. They can also move liquids across the cell's surface.

Coughing and sneezing can be good for you! The mucus in a human's nose and throat trap the bits of dirt and pollution breathed in from the environment. When coughing or sneezing, the cilia move together like a wave to push the dirt-filled mucus out of the airways.

WOW!

The cilia in a person's airways move back and forth about 36,000 times every hour.

See the waves of green and pink in the photo below? These are bronchial cilia. They move bacteria and other particles toward the throat, where you breathe them out!

Types of Cells

There are two main types of **cells**. Scientists use information about the **organelles** a cell has in order to classify it. **A cell without a nucleus and most other organelles is classified as a prokaryotic cell. Cells that contain a nucleus are considered eukaryotic cells.**

Prokaryotic cells

The most significant characteristic of a **prokaryotic cell** is that it does not contain a **nucleus**. Bacteria are prokaryotic cells that live inside humans and all around the environment.

These prokaryotic cells are E. coli bacteria that have been magnified 17,000 times.

Bacteria in action

Some bacteria harm people by causing sickness like food poisoning. Other bacteria can protect humans from infections and help digest food.

Bacteria are also used in environmental recycling and clean-up. Bacteria clean sewage water and make it possible for humans to use it again. The bacteria actually eat the sewage. As the sewage passes through their bodies, it changes into harmless substances. The water can return to rivers without damaging river life.

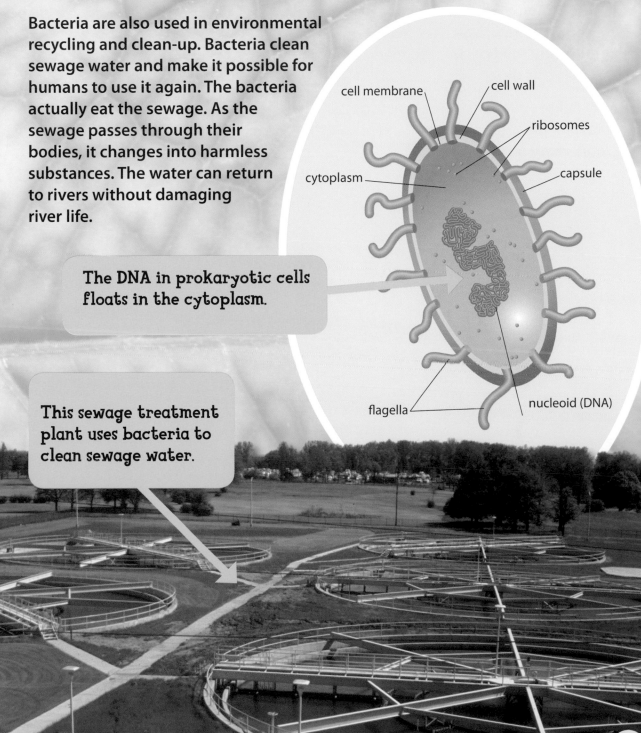

cell membrane

cell wall

ribosomes

cytoplasm

capsule

The DNA in prokaryotic cells floats in the cytoplasm.

This sewage treatment plant uses bacteria to clean sewage water.

flagella

nucleoid (DNA)

Eukaryotic cells

Other than bacteria, all living things in the environment are made up of **eukaryotic cells**. Plants and animals contain many eukaryotic cells. Some fungi such as mushrooms, mold, and mildew are also made of eukaryotic cells.

All eukaryotic cells contain a nucleus. Eukaryotic cells also have a **cytoskeleton** and many other organelles.

Eukaryotic cells are much larger than prokaryotic cells. They also contain a nucleus (below in dark red). This eukaryotic cell has been magnified 24,570 times.

This plane is spraying crops with fungi that kill insects that are harmful to the plants.

Biocontrol

Some eukaryotic organisms are used for pest control! These organisms keep insects from destroying plants that feed and clothe humans. Instead of using chemical poisons, certain fungi are sprayed on the insects in the fields. The fungi eventually kill the insects while keeping the plants safe. This method, called **biological control** (biocontrol), is less expensive than chemical pesticides. Biocontrol also does not put human-made chemicals into the environment.

Organisms

An **organism** is another name for a living thing. Organisms come in many shapes and sizes. All organisms are made up of **cells**. Some organisms contain just one cell. Other organisms have many cells. <u>**All organisms have structures that are organized in ways that allow them to function and survive in their environment.**</u>

Single-celled organisms

What types of living things contain just one cell? **Prokaryotic cells** such as bacteria are single-celled organisms. So are some **eukaryotic cells** such as amoebas. Even a single-celled organism could not survive without being organized. That single cell must have structures arranged so that the organism can move, get food, get rid of waste, and protect itself.

Multicellular organisms

Any living thing made up of more than one cell is a **multicellular organism**. Plants and animals are multicellular organisms. Multicellular organisms usually have more than one type of cell. Different types of cells do different jobs in order for the entire organism to survive.

This amoeba (magnified 85 times) has no brain, but is sensitive to light.

AMOEBA MYSTERY

An amoeba has no brain or ability to feel. Yet the amoeba hates light, especially blue light. If the amoeba is exposed to any light, it will find a shadow and form itself into the shape of that shadow. If an amoeba is exposed to light with no shadows, it will empty out all food and water inside its body and shape itself into a ball.

Scientists do not know how an amoeba can sense light without a brain or nerves. It remains a mystery of nature!

Cells and Energy

How does a **cell** get **energy** to function? There are several sources of energy for cells. <u>All cells can release energy from food molecules. Some cells can also use energy from sunlight to make food.</u>

Energy from food

Humans and animals must consume certain nutrients in food in order for cells to stay healthy. Energy is produced when cells break down and change food **molecules** through **chemical reactions**.

Nutrients	Function	Foods that contain this nutrient
water	Water helps to transport substances throughout the body. Water also keeps cells at a healthy, constant temperature. Most chemical reactions in cells could not take place without water.	apples, celery, lettuce
carbohydrates	Carbohydrates serve as the main source of energy for the body. Carbohydrates also make up many cell parts.	bread, potatoes, vegetables, pasta
fats	Fat molecules store large amounts of energy so cells can use the energy at a later time. **Cell membranes** are made mostly of fats.	olive oil, nuts, salmon, butter
proteins	Proteins are used to build body parts such as muscle, skin, and hair. Every cell contains proteins that speed up chemical reactions in order for the cell to survive.	cheese, eggs, fish, meat, milk

Fermentation

Some cells can get energy from food in a chemical reaction called **fermentation**. In fermentation, food molecules are broken down and energy is released without using oxygen.

In the human body

When a person runs or plays sports hard for a long time, fermentation occurs in the muscles. No matter how fast that person breathes in, the muscle cells use up oxygen faster than it is inhaled. Because the muscle cells must have energy to keep the body moving, fermentation occurs. The muscles make energy from tiny food molecules without using oxygen. Fermentation also produces **lactic acid**. The lactic acid makes muscles feel weak and sore after hard exercise.

As these athletes race around the track, fermentation is occurring in their muscles.

Respiration

When oxygen is present, **cells** gain energy from food through a process called **cellular respiration. During respiration, cells break down simple food molecules and release the energy they contain.**

What do cells need for respiration?

Cells need two materials in order for respiration to take place: oxygen and sugar. The oxygen comes from the air or water surrounding the **organism**. The sugar, or **glucose**, comes from the food the organism eats. However, cells can also use amino and fatty acids, not just glucose.

Bread is one of many foods used by the body to produce energy in cells.

Chemical reaction

The sugar **molecules** are broken down in a chemical reaction requiring oxygen. During this reaction, energy is released. The cell uses this energy to function.

The cell also produces water and carbon dioxide gas as a result of the chemical reaction. These waste products are released from cells into the air and water.

sugar + oxygen = energy + carbon dioxide + water

Breathing and respiration

Cellular respiration is not the same as breathing. Breathing is moving air in and out of the lungs. In contrast, cellular respiration takes place inside cells. It is a series of chemical reactions that turns food into usable energy. Cellular respiration requires oxygen but it does not involve inhaling and exhaling air.

Breathing takes place in the lungs. Cellular respiration happens inside cells throughout the body.

Photosynthesis

Most plants make their own food through **photosynthesis**. <u>In photosynthesis, cells capture energy from sunlight and use it to make sugar.</u> **Cells** use the **energy** in the sugar to carry out important cell functions. Photosynthesis takes place in two stages.

Capturing energy

First, the plant must capture energy from the Sun. This happens mostly in the leaves. A green chemical called **chlorophyll** captures energy from sunlight. It uses it for power in the second stage of photosynthesis.

Making food

In the second stage, the cell uses the energy from sunlight to produce food for the plant. The plant needs two other ingredients for this process: water and carbon dioxide. The plant roots get water from the soil. The carbon dioxide comes from the air.

Once inside the leaves, the energy from the Sun is used to turn the water and carbon dioxide into sugar and oxygen. The plant cells use the sugar for energy to function. The oxygen is released into the air.

Carbon dioxide + water + light energy = sugar + oxygen

Try This!

Cover the solar cells on a solar-powered calculator with your finger. Then, uncover the panel. What happens to the number display? What happens if you only cover part of the panel? What can you infer about the energy that powers the calculator?

Chlorophyll in leaf cells works in a similar way. The chlorophyll captures the light energy and uses it to power the process of making food for a plant.

The cells in these leaves contain chlorophyll, which is important in photosynthesis.

THANK PLANTS!
Be thankful for plants! People need the oxygen released by plants during photosynthesis in order to breathe. Plants take up the carbon dioxide exhaled by humans to make food.

Cell Growth and Division

Each person on Earth started out as a single **cell**. Yet an adult human body contains about 10 trillion cells and is much larger than a baby. How does this growth occur? <u>All living things grow because the cells inside them increase in size and divide to make new cells.</u>

Growing cells

Generally, there is an average size for each type of cell. When a cell reaches the average size of maturity, it divides to make two new cells. These two cells are identical to the original. They then grow and divide again. In this way, new cells are made frequently.

Fertilization

Humans and animals create offspring when the male sperm cell fuses with the female egg cell. This process is called **fertilization**. The single new cell begins to grow and divide almost immediately.

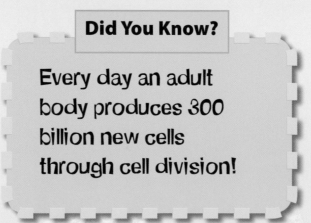

Did You Know?

Every day an adult body produces 300 billion new cells through cell division!

How will this baby eventually become the size of an adult? The answer lies in the processes of cell growth and division.

WOW!

Every human being has spent half an hour as a single cell!

The cell cycle

The regular sequence of growth and division in cells is called the cell cycle. The **cell cycle** begins when a new cell forms. It ends when the cell divides into two identical new cells. The cell cycle happens in three main stages:

STAGE 1
Interphase

During **interphase**, the cell grows, makes a copy of its **DNA**, and prepares to divide into two cells.

STAGE 2
Mitosis

The nucleus divides into two exact copies of the original during **mitosis**. Each new nucleus gets a complete set of DNA.

STAGE 3
Cytokinesis

During **cytokinesis**, the **cytoplasm** divides to form two identical daughter cells. The original cell no longer exists.

After cytokinesis, the cell cycle begins again.

The importance of cell division

Making more cells through cell division allows organisms like plants and animals to grow from babies into adults. Also, old and worn out cells are replaced through cell division. Some cells, such as the ones on the inside of the human stomach, wear out after only a few days. Because of cell division, new stomach cells constantly replace the old ones.

What happens if cells are lost or damaged because of scrapes, cuts, or other injuries? Damaged cells are replaced by cell division. That is the reason a cut on the skin heals over time. New skin cells are made by cell division.

Did You Know?

Without cell division, a human's skin would quickly disappear. People lose about 30,000-40,000 dead skin cells every minute. By 70 years of age, an average person will have lost 105 pounds of skin! Cell divisions constantly replace old skin cells with new ones.

WOW!

Most dust particles inside your house are made from dead skin cells!

The large pink circles (below) are the nuclei of human skin cells.

Specialized Cells

Does a football player look the same as a ballet dancer? Cells that perform different jobs do not look the same either. In a **multicellular organism**, different cells have special features to help them do specific jobs. <u>Cells with unique structures are called specialized cells.</u>

Cell differentiation

How do cells become specialized? Specialization occurs through a process called cell differentiation. The **DNA** in the nucleus contains the instructions of a cell. Nearly all the cells of a multicellular organism contain the same DNA. However, different parts of the instructions in the DNA are used to make different types of cells. The different types of cells have unique features and functions.

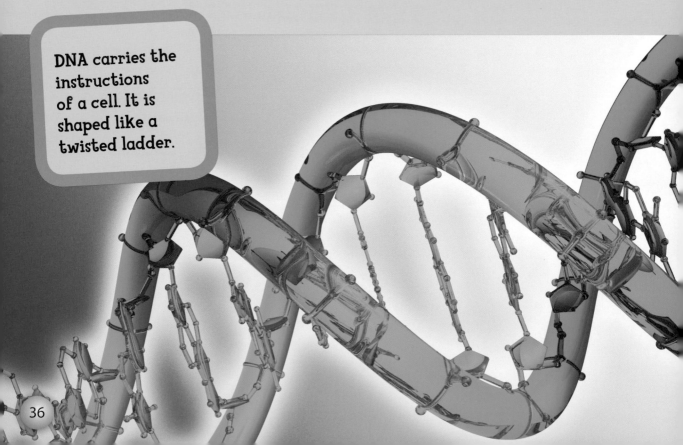

DNA carries the instructions of a cell. It is shaped like a twisted ladder.

Different shapes, different jobs!

Because of cell differentiation, cells have specialized structures and shapes that help them do their jobs. For example, a red blood cell has a flattened, doughnut shape. The large amount of surface area helps this type of cell to pick up oxygen as it moves. The red blood cell is able to perform its job of carrying oxygen around the human body.

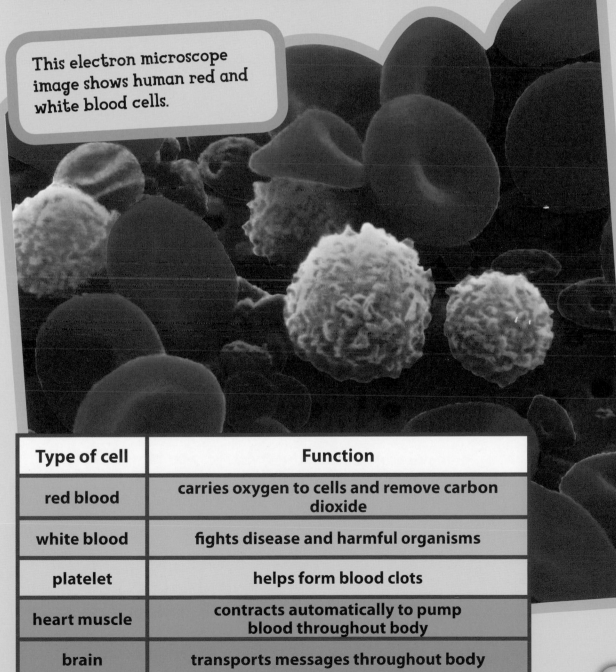

This electron microscope image shows human red and white blood cells.

Type of cell	Function
red blood	carries oxygen to cells and remove carbon dioxide
white blood	fights disease and harmful organisms
platelet	helps form blood clots
heart muscle	contracts automatically to pump blood throughout body
brain	transports messages throughout body

Brain cells

The human brain controls every part of the body. The brain is made of close to 10 billion nerve cells, or **neurons**. Neurons are specialized cells with structures that help them perform the important job of sending and receiving messages in the body.

The special shape of a neuron helps it perform its job in the human brain.

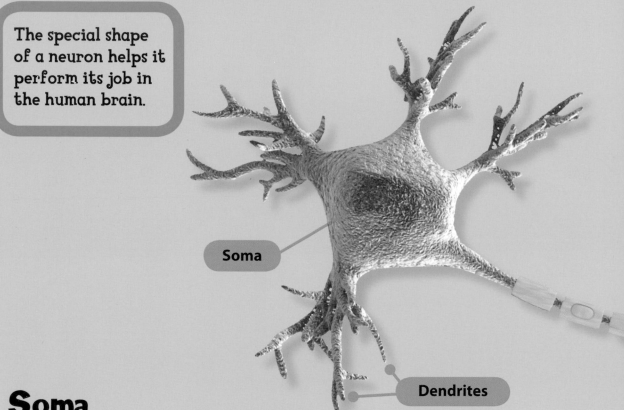

Soma

Dendrites

Soma

The central core of the neuron is called the **soma**. The soma contains the nucleus of the neuron.

Dendrites

The tree-like branches are called **dendrites**. Dendrites receive information from other neurons. Usually, neurons have many dendrites.

WOW!

The human brain cell can hold five times as much information as the Encyclopedia Britannica.

Axon

The long cable-like branch of a neuron is called the **axon**. The axon carries information away from the soma to other neurons. The axon of one neuron lies close to the dendrites of another.

Synapse

The end of the axon contains **synapses**. These are special structures that release chemicals in order to send information to other neurons.

Synapse

Axon

Poisoning the brain

Drinking alcohol affects the neurons in the brain. Alcohol slows down the communication between cells, leading to blurry vision, distorted speech, reduced coordination, and dulled senses. Excessive alcohol in the body can lead to poisoning or death because blood cells stick together and clog the blood vessels. This limits blood flow to the brain.

Various illegal drugs affect brain cells. With repeated drug use, normal systems of communication between neurons change. This breakdown can lead to disruption in concentration, memory, the ability to feel pleasure, and other brain functions. Drugs can cause permanent brain damage.

Stem cells

In humans, most cells cannot become any other type of cell after they differentiate. Neurons will remain neurons, and muscle cells will always be muscle cells. However, there are some cells in the human body that are not specialized. These unspecialized cells are called **stem cells**. Under certain conditions, stem cells can be made to grow into many different types of cells. For example, a stem cell can become a muscle cell, a brain cell, or a red blood cell. Scientists and doctors are researching how stem cells can be used to replace specialized cells that are damaged by certain diseases in people.

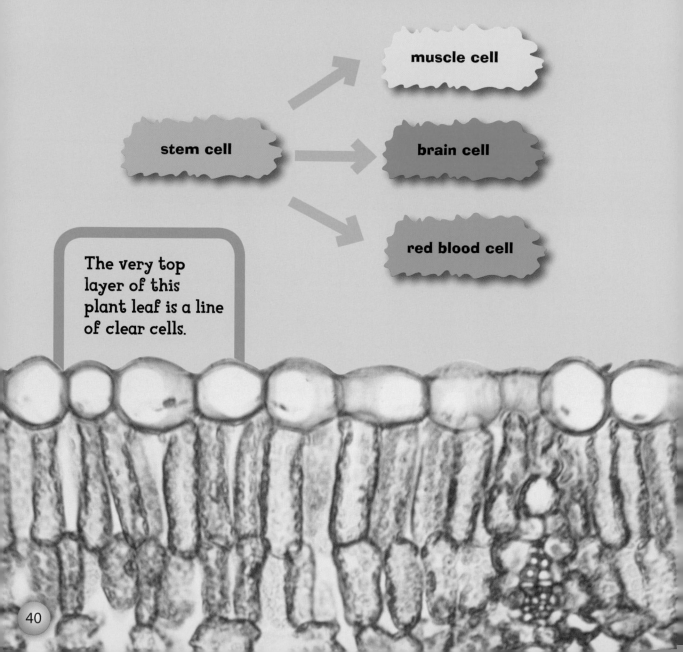

muscle cell

stem cell

brain cell

red blood cell

The very top layer of this plant leaf is a line of clear cells.

Specialized cells in plants

Just like animals, plants develop specialized cells that carry out specific functions. Plant cell differentiation depends mostly on the cell's position within the plant. For example, the upper skin of a leaf contains a single layer of clear cells. These cells allow sunlight through so that it can reach the chloroplasts in the cells below. The cells directly below the clear skin cells in the leaf look like tall columns. They contain many **chloroplasts** for **photosynthesis**. In contrast, the roots of a plant are covered with hair-like cells. These cells have a large surface area that enables the roots to suck up water and minerals from the ground.

This plant root is covered with many tiny hair-like cells.

Cell Function Review

- **Cells** come in different shapes and sizes depending on the job they do.

- The invention of the microscope enabled people to see and learn about cells.

- The **nucleus** of the cell contains **DNA**, the chemical instructions that tell the cell what to do.

- Some cells have **appendages** that enable them to move.

- The **cell membrane** holds the cell together and protects the inside from harmful materials.

- **Eukaryotic cells** have a nucleus; **prokaryotic cells** do not.

- All cells can release energy from food **molecules**. This process is called **cellular respiration**.

- Living things grow because the cells inside them divide to make new cells.

- Specialized cells are cells with unique structures that help the cells do specific jobs.

Quiz

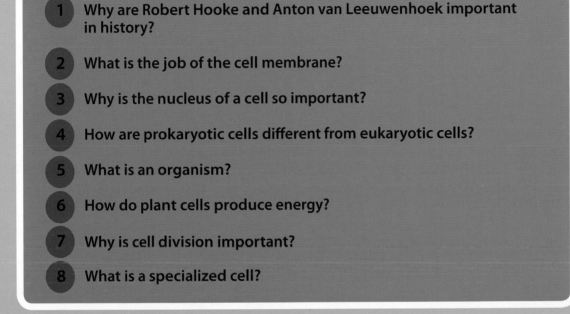

1. Why are Robert Hooke and Anton van Leeuwenhoek important in history?

2. What is the job of the cell membrane?

3. Why is the nucleus of a cell so important?

4. How are prokaryotic cells different from eukaryotic cells?

5. What is an organism?

6. How do plant cells produce energy?

7. Why is cell division important?

8. What is a specialized cell?

8. A specialized cell is cell with a unique structure that does a specific job.

It also replaces old and worn out or damaged cells.

7. Cell division is important because it allows organisms to grow from babies into adults.

6. Plant cells produce energy by a process called photosynthesis. In this process cells capture energy from sunlight and turn it into sugar.

5. An organism is any living thing.

4. Eukaryotic cells contain a nucleus. Prokaryotic cells do not.

3. The nucleus of the cell is important because it contains all of the genetic material for the cell, the instructions that tell the cell what to do.

2. The job of the cell membrane is to protect the inside of the cell from harmful materials.

1. Robert Hooke is important because he was the first person to use the word *cells*. Anton van Leeuwenhoek is important because he was the first person to look to look at single-celled organisms under a microscope.

Answers

43

Glossary

Acoustic microscope A microscope that uses sound waves instead of light or electrons to create an image

Amoeba One of a group of single-celled, animal-like organisms

Appendage An additional structure or part attached to something

Atom The smallest particle of a chemical element that still has the properties of that element. Atoms are considered the "building blocks" of matter.

Axon The long branch of the neuron that carries information away from the soma to other neurons

Biological control The control of pests by interfering with their environment

Cell A tiny unit that is the basic "building block" of life

Cell cycle The regular sequence of growth and division in cells

Cell membrane The thin, flexible covering that surrounds the cell

Cell theory A theory that states that all living things are made of one or more cells, the cell is the smallest unit of life, and all cells are produced from other cells

Cell wall Mostly made of cellulose, this stiff outer layer surrounds the cell membrane. Plants have a cell wall.

Cellular respiration A process by which cells break down simple food molecules and release the energy they contain

Cellulose The tough fibers in the cell wall that give the cell its support and shape

Chemical reaction A process in which one or more substances are changed into other kinds of substances

Chlorophyll The green coloring found inside plant cells that absorbs energy from sunlight for use in photosynthesis

Chloroplast Organelle found within plant cells where photosynthesis takes place

Cilia The tiny hair-like structures that cover some cells. Used for locomotion by some microorganisms.

Cytokinesis The third stage of the cell cycle; in which the cytoplasm divides to form two identical daughter cells

Cytoplasm The jelly-like substance that fills the cell. The parts of the cell are suspended in it.

Cytoskeleton A thick web of fibers that helps the cell keep its shape

Dendrite The tree-like branch of a neuron that receives information from other neurons

DNA (deoxyribonucleic acid) The genetic material of almost all living things. DNA consists of two long chains of nucleotides joined together in a double helix (a shape like a twisted ladder).

Electron One of the very small, negatively charged particles that are a part of atoms, found outside the atom's nucleus

Electron microscope A very powerful microscope that uses electrons (not light) to scan objects

Energy What is produced when cells break down and change food molecules through chemical reactions

Eukaryotic cell An organism made up of a cell or cells that contain a nucleus

Fermentation The process by which food molecules are broken down and energy is released without using oxygen

Fertilization The joining together of a male and female sex cell to produce a new living thing

Flagellum A long, lash-like appendage that serves as an organ of locomotion for some cells including sperm cells

Gene A unit of inheritance passed from parent to offspring

Glucose A type of sugar

Golgi apparatus The part of the cell that stores, changes, and transports molecules received from the RER and the SER

Interphase The first stage of the cell cycle; in which the cell grows, makes a copy of its DNA, and prepares to divide into two cells

Lactic acid Produced by muscle contraction; makes muscles feel weak and sore

Lens Something that focuses rays of light into a sharp image

Mitochondria The power plants of a cell that release energy. They are rod-shaped.

Mitosis A type of cell division where each cell splits to create two identical cells; or the second stage of the cell cycle

Molecule The tiny particle of a substance

Multicellular organism An organism with different cells that have specialized jobs

Neuron A nerve cell

Nucleus The control center of a cell. It contains the DNA.

Organelle One of several different structures, surrounded by a membrane, found in eukaryotic cells. The cell nucleus and plant chloroplast are two types of organelle.

Organism The scientific word for a living thing

Photosynthesis The process by which plants and algae make sugary food using energy from sunlight, carbon dioxide from the air, and water

Prokaryotic cell A cell that lacks a nucleus. All bacteria are prokaryotes.

Protein Substances that make up many cell structures and control a cell's reactions. Proteins are large molecules made up of many subunits called amino acids.

Protozoa (plural for protozoan) Small, single-celled organisms that float around

Ribosome The small structure of a cell that produces protein

Rough endoplasmic reticulum (RER) Located in the cytoplasm, it is a network of tubular membranes involved in transport for the cell; studded with ribosomes

Smooth endoplasmic reticulum (SER) Located in the cytoplasm, it is a network of tubular membranes involved in transport for the cell; smooth surface

Soma The core of the neuron. It contains the nucleus.

Stem cell A cell that keeps the ability to divide and multiply and to create other types of cells

Synapse Special structures at the end of an axon that release chemicals in order to send information to other neurons

Vacuole A chamber surrounded by a membrane, found inside some types of a cell

Further Information

Books to read

Claybourne, Anna. *Microlife: From Amoebas to Viruses*. Chicago: Heinemann Library, 2004.

Houghton, Gillian. *The Respiratory System*. New York: Rosen Publishing, 2007.

Johnson, Rebecca L. *Microquests: Ultra-Organized Cell Systems*. Brookfield, CT: Millbrook Press, 2007.

Meiani, Antonella. *Experimenting with Science: Water*. Minneapolis, MN: Lerner Publications, 2003.

Morgan, Sally. *Cells and Cell Function*. Chicago: Heinemann Library, 2006.

Parker, Steve. *Microlife That Helps Us*. Chicago: Raintree, 2006.

Stille, Darlene R. *Cells*. Strongsville, OH: Gareth Stevens, 2008.

Tesar, Jenny E. *Stem Cells*. San Diego, CA: Blackbirch Press, 2003.

Websites

http://kids.niehs.nih.gov/
This site, sponsored by the National Institute of Environmental Health Sciences, provides lots of kid-friendly links to more science projects, games, activities, and information.

http://www.fsea.org/
Are you a future scientist? Click on the site, and follow the links to discover how you can get involved with science at your school or on the Internet.

http://www.all-science-fair-projects.com/
Are you looking for a really great science project to do for the next science fair at your school? This site provides over 500 free science project ideas. Do some research... maybe you'll find some inspiration for your next great idea!

http://www.madsci.org/
It's the science lab that never sleeps! Ask scientists questions about anything at this fun and colorful site.

http://pbskids.org/zoom/activities/sci/
PBS sponsors this site filled with activities, hands-on projects, and much more.... Covers all types of sciences; from life science to physical science.

http://www.pbs.org/wgbh/nova/baby/divi_flash.html
This site, also from PBS and NOVA, takes you through the steps of mitosis in a colorful and visually-stimulating presentation!

Index

acoustic
  microscopes 9
alcohol 39
amino acids 28
amoebas 24, 25
animal cells 4, 15,
  16, 22, 24, 26, 32,
  35, 41
appendages 18, 19
axons 39

bacteria 15, 20,
  21, 24
biological control 23
blood cells 12, 37,
  39, 40
brain cells 37, 38,
  39, 40
breathing 29

carbohydrates 26
carbon dioxide 28,
  30, 31, 37
cell cycle 34
cell differentiation
  36, 37, 41
cell division 32, 33,
  34, 35
cell growth 32, 33
cell membranes 12,
  16, 26
cell theory 9
cellular respiration
  28, 29
cellulose 16, 17
cell walls 16, 17
chemical reactions
  10, 14, 26, 27,
  28, 29

chlorophyll 30, 31
chloroplasts 14,
  15, 41
cilia 19
classification 20
cytokinesis 34
cytoplasm 10, 14,
  15, 34
cytoskeletons 10,
  15, 22

damaged cells 35,
  39, 40
dendrites 38, 39
discovery 6, 7, 9
DNA 12, 34, 36

egg cells 32
electron
  microscopes 8
energy 4, 14, 15, 26,
  27, 28, 30, 31
eukaryotic cells 20,
  22, 23, 24

fats 26
fatty acids 28
fermentation 27
fertilization 32
flagellum 18
food 14, 15, 21, 24,
  25, 26, 27, 28,
  30, 31

genes 12
glucose 28, 30
Golgi apparatus 15

Hooke, Robert 7, 9

human body 5, 12,
  19, 20, 21, 26, 27,
  29, 31, 32, 33, 35,
  37, 38, 40

interphase 34

lactic acid 27
Leeuwenhoek,
  Anton van 7, 9

membranes. See cell
  membranes.
microscopes 6, 7, 8,
  9, 18
mitochondria 14, 15
mitosis 34
multicellular
  organisms 24, 36
muscle cells 26, 27,
  37, 40

neurons 38, 39, 40
nucleus 10, 11, 12,
  15, 20, 22, 34, 36,
  38
nutrients 26

organelles 14, 20, 22
oxygen 27, 28, 29,
  30, 37

photosynthesis 30,
  31, 41
plant cells 4, 14, 15,
  16, 17, 22, 23, 24,
  30, 31, 35, 41
platelets 37
prokaryotic cells 20,

24
proteins 4, 10, 12,
  14, 26
protozoa 7

respiration.
  See cellular
  respiration.
ribosomes 14, 15
rough endoplasmic
  reticulum (RER)
  15

sewage 21
shapes 4, 10, 15, 16,
  37
sizes 4, 12, 24, 32
skin cells 12, 26,
  35, 41
smooth
  endoplasmic
  reticulum (SER)
  15
soma 38, 39
specialized cells 36,
  37, 38, 40, 41
sperm cells 18, 32
stem cells 40
stomach cells 35
sugar. See glucose.
sunlight 26, 30,
  31, 41
synapses 39

vacuoles 15

waste 15, 24, 28
water 10, 15, 21, 26,
  28, 30, 41